Postcards From P.S. I Love You

Compiled by H. Jackson Brown, Jr.

Rutledge Hill Press
Nashville, Tennessee

Published in Nashville, Tennessee by Rutledge Hill Press, Inc.,
211 Seventh Avenue North, Nashville, Tennessee 37219.
Distributed in Canada by H.B. Fenn and Company Ltd.,
Mississauga, Ontario

Printed in Mexico
1 2 3 4 5 6 7 8 9 — 95 94 93

Introduction

❧

Over the years Mom wrote my sister and me hundreds of letters. What we cherished most were the postscripts she added to each one.

There, in just a few words, she encouraged and inspired us with keen observations, gentle humor, and loving advice.

Some of her P.S. notes were published as a book entitled, *P.S. I Love You*, which became a national bestseller.

This postcard series is based on my favorite entries from the book. Jan and Laurie Ellis, two friends of mine and the art directors for this project, have created beautiful graphic backgrounds for Mom's messages.

As you glance through the collection, I bet you will think of several people who would love to receive an inspiring and encouraging postcard from you. We all know the joy of getting mail that lets us know that we are loved and cherished.

I hope you get a special pleasure mailing these cards. I know the people who receive them will appreciate your thoughtfulness.

HAVE I TOLD

You

LATELY WHAT

A WONDERFUL

PERSON

YOU ARE?

From *P.S. I Love You* by H. Jackson Brown, Jr.
Rutledge Hill Press, Nashville, Tennessee

A small
house holds
just as much love
as a big one.

From *P.S. I Love You* by H. Jackson Brown, Jr.
Rutledge Hill Press, Nashville, Tennessee

If you
don't
have a

Smile

I'll give
you one
of mine.

From *P.S. I Love You* by H. Jackson Brown, Jr.
Rutledge Hill Press, Nashville, Tennessee

Don't do anything that wouldn't make your

MOM

proud.

From *P.S. I Love You* by H. Jackson Brown, Jr.
Rutledge Hill Press, Nashville, Tennessee

Do for others

with no desire of returned favors.
We all should plant some trees
we'll never sit under.

From *P.S. I Love You* by H. Jackson Brown, Jr.
Rutledge Hill Press, Nashville, Tennessee

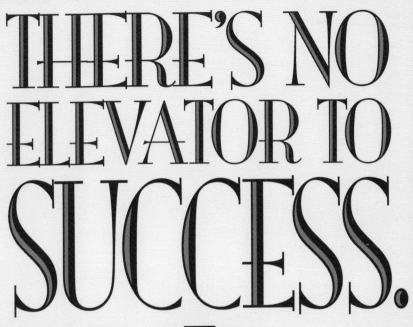

THERE'S NO ELEVATOR TO SUCCESS.

YOU HAVE TO TAKE THE STAIRS.

From *P.S. I Love You* by H. Jackson Brown, Jr.
Rutledge Hill Press, Nashville, Tennessee

Never worry.

❧

Your mother worries enough for both of you.

From *P.S. I Love You* by H. Jackson Brown, Jr.
Rutledge Hill Press, Nashville, Tennessee

If you keep wait-
ing for just the
right time, you
may never begin.

Begin now!
Begin where
you are with
what you are.

From *P.S. I Love You* by H. Jackson Brown, Jr.
Rutledge Hill Press, Nashville, Tennessee

Good
character

is more to be praised than outstanding talent. Most talents are, to some extent, a gift. Good character, by contrast, is not given to us. We have to build it piece by piece—by thought, choice, courage and determination.

—*John Luther*

From *P.S. I Love You* by H. Jackson Brown, Jr.
Rutledge Hill Press, Nashville, Tennessee

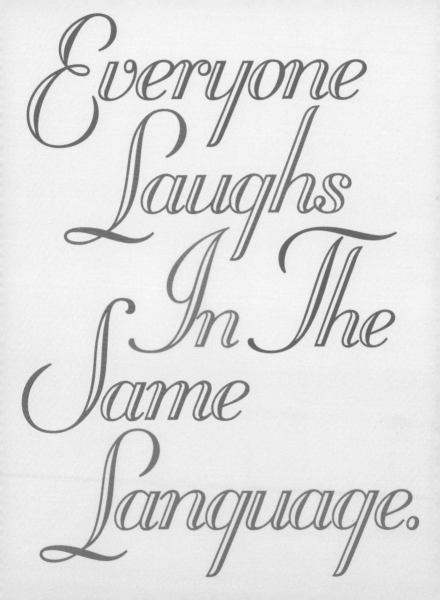

From *P.S. I Love You* by H. Jackson Brown, Jr.
Rutledge Hill Press, Nashville, Tennessee

W

make a living

by what we get.

We make a life by

what we give.

From *P.S. I Love You* by H. Jackson Brown, Jr.
Rutledge Hill Press, Nashville, Tennessee

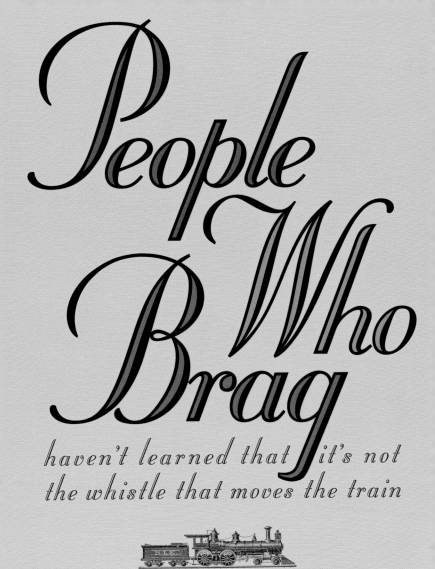

People Who Brag haven't learned that it's not the whistle that moves the train

From *P.S. I Love You* by H. Jackson Brown, Jr.
Rutledge Hill Press, Nashville, Tennessee

Love

Is Never Wasted.

From *P.S. I Love You* by H. Jackson Brown, Jr.
Rutledge Hill Press, Nashville, Tennessee

Today give a stranger one of your beautiful s m i l e s.

It might be the only sunshine he sees all day.

From *P.S. I Love You* by H. Jackson Brown, Jr.
Rutledge Hill Press, Nashville, Tennessee

Twenty years from now you will be more disappointed by the things you didn't do than by the ones you did do. So, throw off the bowlines. Sail away from the safe harbor. Catch the trade winds in your sails. Explore. Dream. Discover.

From *P.S. I Love You* by H. Jackson Brown, Jr.
Rutledge Hill Press, Nashville, Tennessee

DON'T SETTLE FOR SUCCESS WHEN EXCELLENCE IS WITHIN YOUR GRASP.

From *P.S. I Love You* by H. Jackson Brown, Jr.
Rutledge Hill Press, Nashville, Tennessee

The quickest way to make yourself

Happy

is to make someone else happy.

From *P.S. I Love You* by H. Jackson Brown, Jr.
Rutledge Hill Press, Nashville, Tennessee

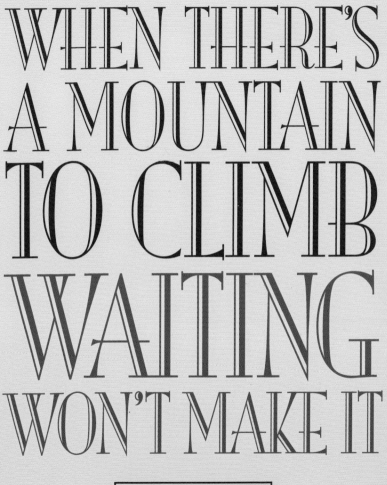

WHEN THERE'S
A MOUNTAIN
TO CLIMB
WAITING
WON'T MAKE IT

SMALLER

Remember the

Golden Rule.

And remember

it's your

turn.

From *P.S. I Love You* by H. Jackson Brown, Jr.
Rutledge Hill Press, Nashville, Tennessee

The smallest act of

KINDNESS

is worth more than

the grandest intention.

From *P.S. I Love You* by H. Jackson Brown, Jr.
Rutledge Hill Press, Nashville, Tennessee

Everyone you meet
knows something
you don't know
but need to know.
LEARN
from them.

From *P.S. I Love You* by H. Jackson Brown, Jr.
Rutledge Hill Press, Nashville, Tennessee

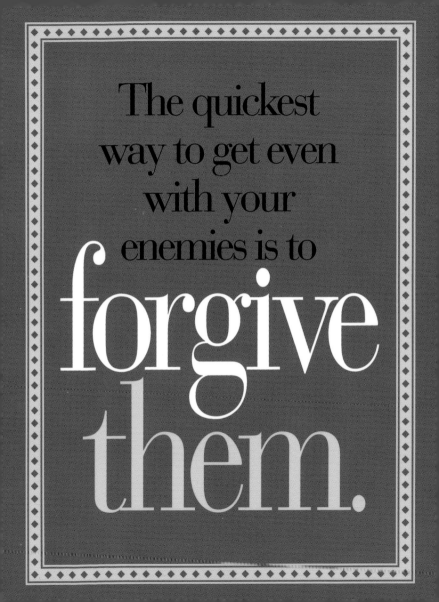

From *P.S. I Love You* by H. Jackson Brown, Jr.
Rutledge Hill Press, Nashville, Tennessee

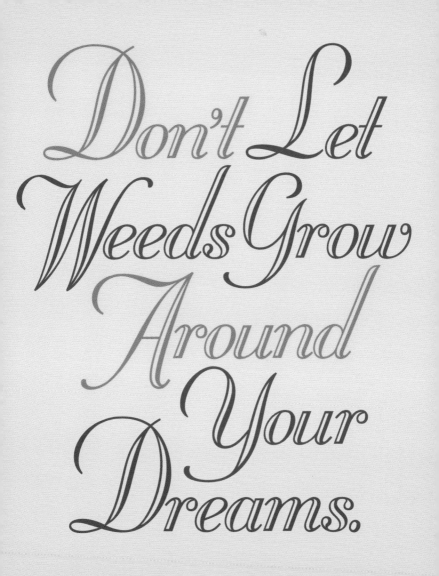

Don't Let Weeds Grow Around Your Dreams.

From *P.S. I Love You* by H. Jackson Brown, Jr.
Rutledge Hill Press, Nashville, Tennessee

Everyone can
afford to be
generous with
PRAISE.

From *P.S. I Love You* by H. Jackson Brown, Jr.
Rutledge Hill Press, Nashville, Tennessee

LOVE

is like wildflowers.

It blooms in the

most unlikely places.

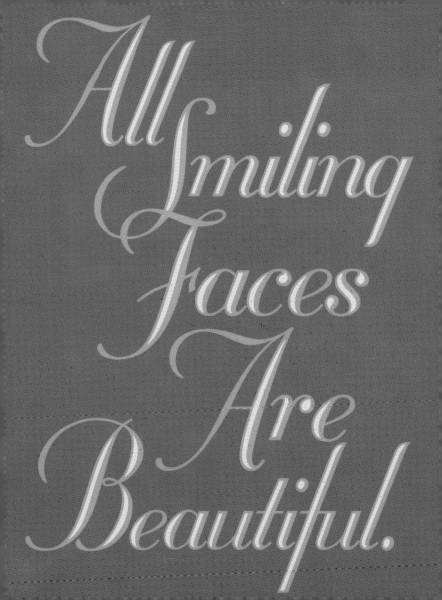

All Smiling Faces Are Beautiful.

From *P.S. I Love You* by H. Jackson Brown, Jr.
Rutledge Hill Press, Nashville, Tennessee

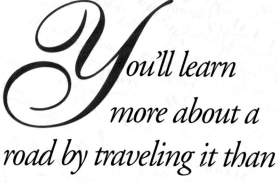

You'll learn more about a road by traveling it than by consulting all the maps in the world.

From *P.S. I Love You* by H. Jackson Brown, Jr.
Rutledge Hill Press, Nashville, Tennessee

TALK

Slow.

THINK

Fast.

From *P.S. I Love You* by H. Jackson Brown, Jr.
Rutledge Hill Press, Nashville, Tennessee

I Love You

THREE WORDS

I Love You

YOU CAN'T HEAR

I Love You

TOO OFTEN OR

I Love You

SAY TOO MUCH.

I Love You

From *P.S. I Love You* by H. Jackson Brown, Jr.
Rutledge Hill Press, Nashville, Tennessee